The Quarry

The Quarry

New Poems

RICHARD EBERHART

NEW YORK

OXFORD UNIVERSITY PRESS

1964

To *Betty, Rick and Gretchen*

Acknowledgments

Some of the poems in this book first appeared
in the following publications, to whose Editors I am grateful
for permission to reprint:

Audience   The Beloit Poetry Journal   The Carleton Miscellany
Encounter (London)   The Green World   Greensleeves
The Hudson Review   The Kenyon Review   The London Magazine
The Massachusetts Review   The Nation   The New-England Galaxy
The New Orland Poetry Anthology, Vol. II   New Statesman and Nation
New Ventures   The New York Review of Books
The Observer   Pennsylvania Literary Review
Poetry (Chicago)   Poetry (London-New York)   Poetry Northwest
The Prairie Schooner   Quarterly Review of Literature
Rhode Island School of Design Alumni Bulletin
Saturday Review   The Sewanee Review   Shenandoah   Syracuse 10
Times Literary Supplement (London)   Transatlantic Review
Whetstone   The Wind and the Rain   The Yorkshire Post

"A New England Bachelor" and "Rainscapes, Hydrangeas, Roses
and Singing Birds" appeared in *Modern American Poetry—Modern
British Poetry* (revised edition), edited by Louis Untermeyer,
Harcourt, Brace and World, Inc., New York, 1962.
The poems "Moment of Equilibrium among the Islands,"
"Sea Burial from the Cruiser *Reve*," and "Vision" appeared
originally in *The New Yorker*.

Contents

Part I

The Kite

I *Sensitivity of the First Flight*

Your blood has coursed and rushed with anticipation.
You have also studied the ratcheted wheels of the reel,
Invested yourself in the rig of the parachute-like harness,
Learned bowline, fisherman's bend, four-strand overhand, larkshead loop.
Already many times tangled in the winding drums
You have exercised exegetical practice on the lines,
Threaded and rethreaded spanwise the spreader bar,
If need be with a twig or straw, by the sea's edge.

II *Theory*

Not like that example showing the absolute mastery of nature
So that if there is wind enough to lift the lovely shape
The same wind turning a vane at the fore
Turns with remitted motion a rudder at the rear,
So back and forth, to right and left, across the sky
Steered by its own motion, the sail must go

With a low, long undulation of precision
Standing into the sky with a sublime indifference
And regularity to the whims that may destroy it,
As if it were its own theory and reason for being

3

Freely the agent of its own pleasing exercise,
Imperturbable before the wind's perturbation,
Nicety, balance and ease of operation; as if
There were order in the universe; as if
Order were in the mind of man,
But as everything is fixed to something
So this air-engine, in an access of cleverness,
Itself moving in azimuth or elevation
Is fixed to light metal rods in the shape of an A,
This fixation the more to unfix our earthless emblem,
For the wind that keeps aloft the sail
And equally sails it slowly to and fro,
The vane being attached by linen cords to the A,
Also deftly marches it on the surface of the ocean,
This free and faultless thing then is a target,
Can be launched from cruiser or battleship,
Will make a deflection target for air gunnery,
Can be shot at by different ships in passing,
The metal floats so cunningly devised
That upon destruction in the air by gunfire,
Or descent of the sail for lack of air-power,
A change of weights and balances opens small holes,
The sea rushes in, the whole engine sinks from sight
Leaving no trace to enemies upon the broad Pacific,
As a dream kept long alive, aloft, in night thoughts
Suddenly disappears from the mind beyond any call.

To be a flier of kites is not the least of my desires!
In this you see the symbol of your relation to the universe;
The wind, unseen, is God, upon which all is dependent,
Sometimes absent, sometimes present, always possible,
In time. The sail, whether in guise of cerulean

Blue make, undistinguishable at a distance from the sky,
Or almost so, as you are from nothingness, in time,
Or almost so, is soul or spirit, yours,
Which you release to flight, which seems to be free,
But over which you hold manoeuverability
Yet it is nothing without the Author of its motion;
Or dotted like a Hamp, a Tony, a Rufe, or Nan
Its suns of rising redness set before the sun's gold eye,
Held thus in the sky to be a mask, the sign of evil,
And save your eye from the true sun's all-inclusiveness,
Else dazzling you, the sun not truly masked,
You lose control, all's gone in a second to wreckage.

If you would look into the sun, put something before it,
Put the mask of evil before it if you can.

Or say the sky is the father-mother symbol, the
Wind is the generator, the lines umbilical,
And you the kite: Fly high, fly low, luff
Or porpoise, or buckle, or break your bonds,
Whether destroyed in the ocean, or destroyed on the sand,
You are not lost, but a part of the world's plan.
It is the sperm searching the great womb of the sky,
Restless with creative energy, flirting with eternity,
Attempting the gift of itself beyond itself,
Dying upon the very air that holds it up,
Pulled down by the harness and the reel.
So our thoughts would transcend themselves
But they are limited to the human.
So our souls would unite with God,
But they are imprisoned by the body.
And our intelligences ever at great play
Assume a certain lightness through the years!

Our wills finally respond to the controls
Of infinite forces as viewless as the wind.

III   *The First Flight, and Later*

Then you carry the great thing down to the sea,
To the sand by the sea, harnessed, weighted with gear,
Your helper-launcher eager as you.
In a basket an extra spool of linen string,   .
A knife, pliers, broad Scotch tape, and a metal box
Brimful of buttons, screw eyes, nuts and bolts, the hardware:
You are the wind's guesser, a neophyte of this element
Seaching a distant flagpole, or smoke, or leaves swishing.

With care the bowing is accomplished, all conditions
According to the book are fulfilled, she stands
Taut and singing and a living thing.
On the broad beach, with gulls and hawks playing
And far above airplanes making other curvets
Now the helper walks with it backward
Two hundred feet as you reel out the double lines,
Your hand on the reel-brake to keep the lines taut.
Then holding it up as the arms will,
The helper obliterated by the enormous emblem before,
You test the lines for equal tension,
With horizontal motion of the flying bar
Flap the rudder, when all is ready
As you think, and you are all wary, signal "Up Sail."
Straight up with grace incomparable rising
To high center the kite goes sailing and shining.
In your heart and in your hands are triumph.
Long care you have exercised, long patience,

6

And you think you have cunning.
Such contending as this is in the unpredictable.
The high quiring! Classless you are clumsy,
In a trice it loops over and crashes down,
Instantly inert; broken on the beach.

Quickly dashed this sail, delicate as sensation.

Inspecting the wreckage, you search the cause.
Was it lack of knowledge, or the wind's cantankerous veer?
Then you excise the broken spar, put in a spare,
Make with greater caution and wariness another attempt.

The second time she goes up ten feet
Whirls over and is dashed to pieces in sand.
Again you make necessary repairs,
Baffled by the testy, bluffy bird.

The flier will practice by the hour, and achieve
Slowly the relaxed ease of his controlling motions,
Slowly he will learn the habits of the sail's tactics,
And soon respects the grandeur of the wind's potentiality.

With diligence, the hours flying away in exhilaration
The flier will learn the secret of anticipation
So that the unforeseeable future of the kite's motion
Is the guide of the present instant's motivation;
Unless this is accomplished disaster is imminent!

Then the dominating shape, sturdy in the sky,
Well-weathered and living in its keen nature,
Responsive to the controlled will of the flier
Will be seen to make slow arcs across
The sky's quarter, or hover far over into
The wind, slowly descending, or will rush

7

Up bright to high center, or be compelled
Crabwise across to its last inch of wind-take,
Or perform complete circles to right or left,
Or dazzle the eye in a spectacular figure eight,
Lastly even diving from zenith to,
Almost to earth! reseated upward
Even ten feet before seeming crash to earth
By dexterous, subtle motion of the flying bar!

Much depends upon how much throat you give it,
How it will fly. The slightest adjustment
Of the larkshead loop, will tell. What I call
Open-throated rides against the wind,
Is best in a thirty knot wind for power dives,
But close-throated turns less face to the wind,
Rides more nearly atop it, is gentle sailing,
But that it comes almost overhead porpoising
Which, then, compels correction.

It is possible to dispense with the reel,
To go with no harness, by primitive means
For a flight, having constructed a stick,
Even a broomstick, as a flying bar,
One linen line attached to each end,
The strings wound around as on a bobbin.
This gives for quicker action than the other,
The kite is harder to control, more adventuresome to fly,
Will outhand you in an instant
If you are not continuously concentrating;
Is hard to bring in, but with lucky skill
Can be landed by a forward rush to drop it.

IV *The Wind as an Abstract God*

Every day one looks for the signs of the wind,
Which has now become a living thing, obsessive,
Thought of in terms of sail-lifting pleasure,
A rustle in the holly trees; will it be
Enough? The flag is always indicating,
At the Cavalier. Often in excess of elan
You have tromped all your gear down to the beach
In the anticipation of eight knots, or
Taken the smooth seven-footer that will sail in six,
Its pale blue cover to go slowly and stately,
But by this token it is also less manoeuverable.

Your knowledge of the wind was faulty, and even
Though there is wind at the edges of the waves
Your helper lifts aloft, and you reel in hard,
But the kite will not rise, falling, unbroken.

The fascination of the thing is in the wind!

Sometimes sailing, the kite well exercising,
The wind will drop, and nothing can be done
Nothing, nothing.
You go, with all your gear, reluctant, home.

And you had learned obedience to nature,
Desirous man, had learned obedience to nature,
Before you sulked home with your sticks and fabrics.

V *Adventure on Sunday*

By the seashore, by the Hotel Splendide
When days were on the flame, but lessening
And would not kill the skin with stings,

9

But far enough away, quite far away,
But by the house that read "No Trespassing,"
Not once, but each ten feet upon the jetty,

That house that held a terrible old lady
Whom Furies drove to such a loneliness
She picked up sticks upon the sand all day,

By dawn, and equally in amber evening
She'd rake the sand for any obstacles
But sand, by hand, upon her eminent domain,

Yet dawn the sea dragged in obstreperous foray
And night would overwhelm her restless energy
With wreckage, sea's greenery, a lungfish, a great booby.

Then retreating farther down the beach
In an access of politic prehension,
A pontiff wind available, you come

To the tasks of assembly and adjustment,
Of balancing, and testing, and pre-correction,
To attempt the launching of the vane alone.

By resting the sail on its side on the sand
It is possible to run out the lines, then even them
And reel in until pressure brings it edge up.

Then with swift reel-in off she takes
Laterally and if adroitly handled evenly
Crabs across up and soon seeks high center.

The wind now ardent, you reel out
Letting the wind take it, back, until flapping,
Then put on the brakes to tauten it up.

Then let her go again in opulence of motion
The plane growing smaller, shrinking bright,
And still you let it out, and out, and out,

Noting the gradual slowing of the controls,
The time-lapse in the reaction of the strings
As these gleam deep, in deep unequal curves

Flashing white against the blue, but lost far up.
And you are strong in a springy disrelation
Almost divorced from the plane you control.

It must be almost over the Hotel Splendide!
It must be out almost two hundred yards.
It is tugging on the harness, lustily,

When, pong! the plane loops down under
In a huge circle, comes up, loops over,
Begins another descent, you reel in, run back,

She barely comes up, she goes up over,
Something has snapped, you try for control,
She goes way down under, the thing is giddy,

You barely get her up, each circle losing
Altitude, is altogether behaving crazily,
You reel in frantically. O way down

She goes, she has gone way way down
Out of sight behind the terrible lady's house,
Both lines are hung up over the roof.

It would be the "No Trespassing" house!
Friends come; all assess the situation.
Strangers appear, gazing at the strange gear.

It is not an inconsiderable problem,
The lines are caught hard on the roof. Will
Anybody appear, from the house? You seriously care.

Eventually a sort of council of war.
Actually a calculation of strategy
Upon an attempt at the extravagant.

Another five-footer is put together.
Will the wind hold? Will it work?
Every effort to free the lines has failed.

The reel is wound in to the edge of the lot,
The lines just taut to the top of the roof.
The new kite is held by its delicate bridle,

Each end of the bridle secured to a reel-line
And the idea is to fly the fouled lines off!
"Up Sail." Up she goes heavy and cranky

Carrying the burden of the lines beyond her,
Seeming to refuse, but rising queerly,
Now at the housetop, and now higher rising

The stuck lines are lifted gently away
The useful kite then steered to the beach,
Landed safely to the delight of beholders.

Before which the Jap was thrashing around in the parking lot,
Illogical plaything of partial-fitting wind,
Restrained by dead lines fixed to the roof.

High in air, a tiller-line snapped out a spar eyelet.

VI   *Aerialism*

A whole day of sailing is delight!
Or a day of intermittent sailing and lazing,
For you can find a cove among the dunes
Back a distance from the surf's gift,
In broad view of the expansive Atlantic,
For the repair of kites, or rest between ventures,
With friends, or alone. All day the wind tussles,
Or sometimes it will sink for an hour,
Or rise puffy: there, shielded, on tan grass
Pointed inland by months of wind-rush,
You study the texture of the sail's make,
Rig the lines, attend to checks and balances,
Repair a rent with Scotch tape, barefoot.

To sail by the sea pleases inly
When the wind comes onto the shore
In great staves like music
Playing against your muscles to the orchestrated,
Intricately shifting movements of the vane.
Then it is to test the far-out motion,
Facing to the South, to fly the lines over,
To fly the kite out over the ocean,
Four hundred feet out, say, the wind
Sagging the lines between you and it,
So that there is a certain peril in the control
By time-lapse; also the edge of the wind
May endanger, by lack of its steadiness,
The intrusive tactic into the wind.

By now tipped over, the mast almost horizontal,
You edge it up wind as far as it will go,
With skill try to keep it motionless and still,
Then, with a sense of shearing the minimum,
By forcing it just to horizontal, O be deft,
Down almost to the very touch of the waves
You love to let it.

If disaster results, you rush to the scene,
Try to catch the swamped bird on the in-come,
It must be caught before the last breaker
For the last breaker invariably breaks it up.

Then another attempt of similar aviation.
This time more safely not over the ocean,
You try, by the same minute hand motions,
Trying to gauge errors of the wind's differential,
To land the kite upwind on the beach.
Often like the most skittery bird,
Impatient as a spirit, an earthless thing.
"Light as the wind," the lithe being of the kite
Will dance with an enthralling delicacy,
Just at the touch, or less than touch, of the sand,
Straining and quivering to be up, flirting,
A creature of the completest absence of mind,
An elemental spirit, soul of the graceful.

Then a practiced hand, tightening the controls,
Can bring the full vigor of upward compulsion.

Evening flight makes evening an advancer,
Too soon an all darkener. But you stand there

14

When you can hardly see what you are doing,
O metaphysical adventure!

Until the moon arises,
And you can mask it.

O strange and impalpable evanescence
To be flying by the light of the moon,
With dark-adapted eyes, but uncertain
At any instant what your relation
To the sail is, or how to maintain it,

As it is always with us and reality,
In the eccentric heart of philosophy,

Surely this supposition of control
Yet without certainty of the control

Is where nature has us,
And we have set our minds

For centuries up in the heavens
Where they fly, secreted, dark,

Riding on the winds of chance.

The Spider

I

The spider expects the cold of winter.
When the shadows fall in long Autumn
He congeals in a nest of paper, prepares
The least and minimal existence,
Obedient to nature. No other course
Is his; no other availed him when
In high summer he spun and furled
The gaudy catches. I am that spider,
Caught in nature, summer and winter.
You are the symbol of the seasons too.

II

Now to expatiate and temporize
This artful brag. I never saw so quieting
A sight as the dawn, dew-clenched foot-
Wide web hung on summer barn-eaves, spangled.
It moves to zephyrs that is tough as steel.
I never saw so finely-legged a creature
Walk so accurate a stretch as he,
Proud, capable, patient, confident.
To the eye he gave close penetration
Into real myth, the myth of you, of me.

16

III

Yet, by moving eyesight off from this
There is another dimension. Near the barn,
Down meadow to shingle, no place for spiders,
The sea in large blue breathes in brainstorm tides,
Pirates itself away to ancient Spain,
Pirouettes past Purgatory to Paradise.
Do I feed deeper on a spider,
A close-hauled view upon windless meaning,
Or deeper a day or dance or doom bestride
On ocean's long reach, on parables of God?

The Place

I

Eventually one finds
There is no environment
Patent for the poetic.

Any place will do.
Alas! One thought of a gold
Hullabaloo, a place of glass

Refinement with subtleties
Crossing the transparency
As lively as mind's images.

One thought of a vast portico
With appropriate, energized
Gods and beings, rich purposes.

Alas! Any place will do.
There is no poetical place,
America continues its practices.

Final toughness of the word,
The word bawling imperfections,
Its paradox to be heard.

II

There used to be
The violent struggle
For place, the right

Place poetic in countries
Or cities or underground,
The right place

Was thought emergent
And to harbor you,
Hello! Poetry Place.

The subconscious was
Nearest, perhaps dearest,
Anyway sheerest

But always fleering off.
Ways you went! Allurement
In echoic happiness.

There was no place for poetry.
Entrenched, my flesh is
Poetry's environment.

Sea-Ruck

Washback of the waters, swirl of time,
Flashback of time, swirl of the waters,

> *Loll and stroke, loll and stroke,*

The world remade, the world broken,
Knocked rhythm, make of the slime,

The surge and control, stroke of the time,
Heartbreak healing in the grime, and groaner

Holding its power, holding the hurl,
Loll and hurl, power to gain and destroy,

> *The tall destruction not to undo*

A saffron inevitable sun, far and near,
Some vast control, beyond tear and fear,

Where the blood flows, and nights go,
Man in his makeshift, there is home,

And the dark swells, the everlasting toll,
And being like this sea, the unrolling scroll,

> *Stroke and loll, loll and stroke, stroke, loll*

The Hamlet Father

When Hamlet had sunk to the moist ground
With his most meanings tossed
Back to the unwilling, pregnant sky,
His will and green questions lost,

I thought I had outlived his mark,
Viewing him with thanks and saying,
Hamlet, you are too young to count,
I assign you to the philosophical dark.

Mine are less modest and princely
Lucubrations on the same events.
I am your father and would care
To have richer evidence.

But had you lived longer and deeper
You might have gained a passion
Profound as the master of yours
And lived in a different fashion.

Four Exposures

1. Playful birches in the
      Where the mind goes off in austerity
          Taking the baby to the doctor
   :Flexions
Impressions:
The late quartet draws the heart out
      Cash the check in the morning
          Polio may be latent for years
             Improvisations:
             Destinies
The sun kills as it blesses
      King Canute knew the tides' tactics
          Mallarmé was foolish in his lectures?
             :Seizures,
             Creations:
Never to be serious! Let the jest
      Be on one. And no more philosophy,
          Know more. Will Star's pups be thorough-
          bred, or mongrel?
             :Plumbers,
             Carpenters:
How the world runs to worldliness.
      Strength of the soul! Passionate devotion!
          Go and get honey rolls and streptomycin.
             Hush-a-bye
             Hush-a-bye

2. Rich in dextrins, maltose and dextrose
     And nobody knows the answers. Here
          Comes Aurelia, with the baby carriage
:Dissemble
Invade:
Once having learned Chinese their subtlety
     In linguistic inspissates our English.
          Indian music babyfies J. Bach.
:Pretend, and
Invent:
Twice Washbowl our Cape cat had kittens
     In the same closet. At four of the morning
          She mews, and I let her in the window
               :Salutations
               Historicities:
Shall I allude to Mrs. Phineas Cuff?
     Everybody has a mad neighbor.
          Keep your dog from hence, we have a mummy
               :Bosch
               Angelus Silesius:
They have no bock beer this year.
     Pale genius is burning the midnight oil
          The literary politicians are giving out the prizes
               :Petrifactions
               Liquefy!

3. I dickered with the truth, because
                The truth dickered with me. Fractious
                    Divagations please the senses
            :Presentiments
        Hallucinations:
        Old years laugh hysterically
                At the seriousness of the new.
                        We have seen too much of death in our time.
            :Calculations,
        Fervors:
        If of anything we were intellectually certain
                We could not afford the luxury of the pit.
                    We would be lost in the found.
                            :vastness,
                        Unfound me:
        The source is newness evermore uncreate!
                It is delicious hardship to steal out of it!
                    It is handsome to handle the eventuating.
                            :Gusto
                        Diamonds:
        The baby with her goddess-descending smile then.
                Why not? Others have felt it before.
                    This assurance beyond us from the skies.
                            :Taken up
                        Defended:

4. The worst then ever the best. No defeat
        That is not a subtle victory.
                No victory that is not a defeat.
    : Accept
    Listen:
    It always disturbed me that Job
        Gave up his boils. I see now that tragedy
            Is good only in a certain framework.
                    Shakespeare stops.
                    Homer goes on.
    Birds on the boughs, lovers in the haystacks,
        Cadillacs, Fords, and cold-water flats.
            Lovers couple the theory and the fact.
                    : Vigor
                    fashion:
    Time is the soul's macaronic specialist.
        As the wheel turns, what will come of the wheel?
            What songs, what waters, as the wheels turn?
                    : Trial
                    Aptitude:
    I should have thought the senses best.
        Let Plato, let Aristotle lie.
            Lie to me then in the white night
                    Lover
                    and bride.

La Crosse at Ninety Miles an Hour

Better to be the rock above the river,
The bluff, brown and age-old sandstone,
Than the broad river winding to the Gulf.

The river looks like world reality
And has the serenity of wide and open things.
It is a river of even ice today.

Winter men in square cold huts have cut
Round holes to fish through: I saw it as a boy.
They have a will to tamper with the river.

Up on the high bluffs nothing but spirit!
It is there I would be, where an Indian scout was
Long ago, now purely imaginary.

It is a useless and heaven-depended place,
Commodious rock to lock the spirit in,
Where it gazes on the river and the land.

Better to be rock-like than river-like;
Water is a symbol will wear us all away.
Rock comes to the same end, more slowly so.

Rock is the wish of the spirit, heavy symbol,
Something to hold to beyond worldly use.
I feel it in my bones, kinship with vision,

And on the brown bluffs above the Mississippi
In the land of my deepest, earliest memories,
Rushing along at ninety miles an hour,

I feel the old elation of the imagination.
Strong talk of the river and the rock.
Small division between the world and spirit.

Impatience as a Gesture of Divine Will

Unmasking the self, impatience yielded
To none over alert decades,
Where the steeple stood, and the people
Rose and fell where roses fade.

Life was stampede and ruction.
In the splendid Sunday bustle
The evidence was newly understood,
Yet impatience ruled the roost.

In terror sit, sit down and listen
At the great groan of authority,
Then escape down lissome ways
Sitting in electric eventide.

In fine revolutions of the mind
Spin on, where the spirit breaks
Its great sequestering question
Against your individuality.

Loss

(To V. R. Lang)

Her loss is as something beautiful in air,
The mysterious part of personality
Become the blue mystery of the air,
The far and the near.

In life she had laughter and acting.
She made things gay and severe.
The world continues, beyond reason to fashion,
The far and the near.

She took many parts, she had only one,
One was her sureness of being.
The others were maskings of dark and light,
Her feminine grace of seeing.

I do not know how to say no
To time that goes in any case,
Do not know how to explain
The pure loss and vision of her face.

Contemplation

If I ask my own questions, life gives me
My own answers, despite systems, or prejudices.
I am a defier of times and of treacheries,
A naked man in sunlight, clothed in radiance
Who, sun-fired, is not afraid of the dark
Night of the soul, nor of the hot blast of reason,
But lives to dance in his own imagination.
Individuation is the way to the universal,
Love is the symptom of life's energy,
Hatred, malice and blackness represent
Negative states, but sun-fire is approbation
Esteeming the heavenly in the soul of man
When it is active in positive affiliation.
Acceptance is the beginning of wisdom.
The wise man throws bolts of light about the world
From divinations given him in secret sendings.
As spirit lets spirit flow without hindrance,
Love is an active principle of communion
And the stars, beyond death and beyond life,
Descend, and sparkle, and are a heavenly emblem
Infusing the flesh with peace and prophecy,
Elemental harmony, grand and paternal.

Clocks

I opened a delicate, French metal box
Careful lest I should give nicks or knocks
To one of the most cheerful looking of clocks—

Wondering what was the nature of time,
What it had to do with the nature of rhyme—

When out of this metal case stepped a fairy
As milky white as if out of a dairy
And looked me straight in the eye, very airy.

To Auden on His Fiftieth

Dear Whizz, I remember you at St. Mark's in '39,
Slender, efficient, in slippers, somewhat benign,

Benzedrine taker, but mostly Rampant Mind
Examining the boys with scalpel and tine.

I recall the long talk and the poems-show,
Letters sprinkling through the air all day,

Then you went down and put on Berlioz,
Vastly resonant, full of braggadocio.

I look at your picture, that time, that place,
You had come to defend in the American scene

The idea of something new; you had the odd face
For it, books sprawling on the floor for tea.

It was the time of the *Musée des Beaux Arts*,
Your quick studies of Voltaire and of Melville,

In the rumble seat of my old green Pontiac
I scared you careening through to Concord.

And one time at a dinner party, Auden,
You wolfed your meal before the others were served

Treating the guests to an Intellectual Feast
Probably better than any of us deserved.

I remember your candor and your sympathy,
Your understanding, your readiness, your aliveness,

Your stubby fingers like lightning down the pages;
Our ensuing American years that made you thrive.

Now you are back at Oxford, an Oxford don,
Half a century gone into the Abyss of Meaning.

Here's my well-wish on your fiftieth,
You flex a new twist to the spirit's feigning.

To Bill Williams

I would make this all as single as a song,
My own assumption in a flittering stance,
Twenty years cast in an easy affirmation.

The truth is there is truth on every side,
Each protagonist as relativist
Invests the present with his intellectual twist.

You are no absolute, Bill! But genial soul
And spanking eye, no hatred of your fellows,
Concludes we love you the worldly American.

With gusto to toss the classics out, and with them
The sonnet, you live yet in a classic Now,
Pretend to advance order in your plain music,

And even preach that Form (you call it measure,
Or idiom) is all, albeit your form would mate
The sprawling forms, inchoate, of our civilization.

Nexus

The dead are hovering on the air,
So real they have their flesh and bones.
They appear as they had been,
And speak with firm, daytime tones.

I say, I cannot believe your power.
Go back into the ancient times.
The sun burns on my forehead now,
And thought comes in a spring of rhymes.

My love is like the blue of the air,
My son and daughter play at games.
We live in a yoked immediacy,
Imagination come, that no one tames.

Everything I do today
Moves with a stealthy, spirit strength,
A thrust into the future order,
But yet it has a backward length.

The dead are playing about my head
As real as present, effable air.
They have their power to make and shape
Each breath I take, each thought today.

Examination of Psyche:
Thoughts of Home

Now at ninety this frail and lightsome woman
Goes to the hospital to meet her death.
The long decades stretch as a panorama
And I think of a slow third of a century
She has lived beyond the one I loved.
The one I loved has long since gone to dissolution.
The bare perplexity astounds me still,
How all that love she bore me, and I returned
Fullfold in fond, filial devotion
Saw but shadowy reflection in this other.
Yet beautiful she is, always a reminder,
A triumphant form, statement of life's harmony.
Now at last this delicate-boned, fair woman
Goes toward her death and makes one ponder
On fortune's intricate ways; childless she goes,
Who lived out almost a full century,
In one town, among certainties and changes.
When the mind is ravaged by thought
There is no virtue in the passage of time.

Is there a new myth to people the mind's eye?
Is there a splendor undreamed of by man?

I ask these questions in the name of love
Bestriding life. I think of a delicate-boned woman
In her long, harmonious relationships
Which put off answers to intolerable questions
Assailing me with that other, her friend,
Long lost in the wry, unanswerable enigmas,
And in the name of spirit, likewise bound
On a quest for an ultimate answer,
Here in mid-dream, big and hardy, but alone,
Let me make an epiphany for the living,
For those who die early, for those who die late.

The Record

Reading the stars' epitaphy
I foredeemed empathy.
My hands were free,
Lined with sensuality.

Looking in the spring of the palm
I could perpetrate there without qualm;
All was calm,
Against breakneck violence, balm.

It was up in the stars' periphery
I read the soul's history
And victory,
The voyage of the soul's periptery.

I had enjoined the battle of being
In harshness of inner seeing,
Never fleeing
The antique duties of self-freeing.

Man, what was man, was
Man the ultimate cause
Of all laws,
The old game and the taws?

Laid up, elect, the ideational
Stars were sensational
And passional
Variations of the natural.

I would never descend to man
Without feeling ascend I can
And am
Ascentional by august plan.

Better to live in the higher light
Beyond animal fight,
Night—
Free from dualistic force and blight,

And in true sensuality
Discover the nativity
And history
Of the soul among its immortalities.

39

Divorce

The rock that withstands man's arrogance
Is nature's own rock high above the land;
Lofty in the fogs; pure height on walking days,
Something to look at with an aspiring eye.
Yet never its greatness and true strength
Appear until new divorce breaks old forms.
We do not possess it any more,
Not at all, the forms are ruined by arrogance,
Parents and children are sundered by separation.
Life sprawls in unkempt acres.
It is then the rock stands triumphant, beyond man's
Pride that kept him from a noble union
With nature as he was united with his kind;
But divorce separates us also from the rock.

The Project

The mail box, the roadway, and the dump truck
   a day in June blue and gold

The play rock, the high swing, the pine stand
   a race of children readying time

A prospect of a legendary Connecticut
   angler flicking his fly in amber evening

Tumble of waters at Diana's pool
   Dive, shimmer and roil of bathers, devotees.

It is the pageant of the American summer
   Blue, gold, and high, an elegance of time.

When freefoot lads find a decaying animal
   In the woods, one yells "Help! Don't breathe it!"

The Mother Part

I

I'll never, never learn my art
Though summer the song singer send
Speckling the lance light all in a dart
    and blush my forearm with my big fingers.

I'll never, never learn my quizzical
Heart, not *dame de noche, cadena d'amour*
Hurtle into the nostrils burgling the years,
    nor gash the red flannel from the mouth of the muskallonge.

I'll never, never learn my malleable
My mind, that hearkens to the feather's fandango,
Or leaps the backs of tittles all the air
    about a sweet or savage journey thither.

Such desperation as some lunacy foretells
That's built upon strong vaults of reason
Is like to pulses on the high eye,
    and choking order sweet and maniacal.

In lists of love, in sibylline fictive whispers,
In childhood's fierce career, where cataracting trees
Slice over the head as in the lightning's stroke,
    where werewolves, where gloomy waterfalls,

Or dreads of pustulant August pools;
Where icecakes creak to grind you under the milldam,
Snowstorms like books will stack you up in death;
    or climb a tombstone helmeted with pelvis of a cow;

Or the galled great chain on chaingang in the anchorhold
To sink you through the China sea; the pest of
Fear in a nipa hut that's Filipino flesh,
    or Indian Ocean blistering teacher heat—

     If I could, if feeling could, if the mind could—

Memory, godlike size, incorruptibility,
Be mothering; threads and beats hoard up, draw all
High daylight down into vowel's lucid reaches
    and strength of all our days' imaginings.

Suffer yourself to be apostasized,
But sweet and single hearted memory,
Gambit of time, soul saver, visionary glass,
    redemptive essence of the world's whole, man's loss.

Be girl-footed, adaptable as air,
Be silent, a green faced Buddha of the Bo tree,
An eagle, a great reach for a little prize;
    or seeless whelk the slow Pacific sweeping.

I'll never, never learn my art,
I'll never learn the mother part,
But save me, song, and sing me, summer,
    Incorporeal the time be, the time is inner.

II

Verged are the world's disparities,
The age that now the atom twists to fall,
Haggard Adam and Eve see their garden Hell,
Satan laughs. Christ's arms fling out His cross.

The dead boys are oxydizing by the million;
Hatred, great-swilled throbber, when will
You be shamed out of the world; swill you ever?
His will. The paradox of God Almighty.

    What have I done, what have I done
    That I cannot find what I should have done?

I'll learn my art, I'll learn my art,
Mind and heart are forced apart.
I'll speak in sentiency of mystery,
The truth of loss, for art is home.

Matador

It is because of the savage mystery
There in the coffin, heaved on burly shoulders,
At five o'clock in an afternoon of jostling sunlight,
We wake to the rich meaning of necessity

Close to the horns, on the horns of the dilemma
Instantly tossed, gored by the savage animal,
The dance in the bullring flares sense magnified,
And turned and tended to the pains of perfection.

Matador of the spirit, be you also proud and defiant
By grace and skill, accost hot sunlight without fear,
Try nearer to the fetish tossing of the horns,
Relaxed power best defies the brutal adversary.

And hold that skill most dear that most dares,
The dance almost motionless, as the beast passes,
At five o'clock in an afternoon of jostling sunlight.
Were crowds, and banners, wilderness, and music.

45

Prometheus

Touched by fire,
Holding the light in my hand,
Brilliant-colored October,
Adoration is the only word.

Breathless I am,
I hold the light in my hand,
The red, the green, the tawny,
Blue sky illimitable,
Adoration is the only word.

The light is on my hand,
Changeless golden afternoon,
Gift of the metaphysical,
Deep infusion of the seen,
Adoration is the only word.

And adoration is the only word
As, holding the light in my hand,
The light is on my hand,
Striking dumb,
Touched by fire.

Part II

Old Tom

An old, black, rutting tomcat,
The brother of his female,
Expressed nature in his sister
Begetting again his future.

I eye this old, mangy fellow
With a certain sympathy.
His progeny already
Have suffered fortune and misfortune

Teaching us, as larger animals,
Something of ourselves.
As poets will to survive,
Cats survive by force.

A kitten could not be expected
To understand a moving car.
One, atop my front wheel,
Was rolled down to mutilation.

I had to kill her with a club
And buried her in the bushes,
Shaking with the dread of this
But doing it nevertheless.

Her little brother very soon
Had caught a bird so beautiful
I hated to see it mutilated,
And left only feathers and the spleen.

They are the most civilized creatures,
Sleep all day and hunt by night,
Elegance in the drawing room,
Merciless in dusk or in moonlight.

But most it is their indifference
To death of their own fellows
I applaud; they go about their business,
Unquestioning the fates of those fellows.

Old Tom, here is a handout,
Some meal and some milk for you.
Go rough it under the stars,
You teach us what we are

When our policies are riven
And our pretentions are bare,
And we are subservient to nature
Very much as you are.

The Height of Man

I am where the bluebell dies
But I, where Western storms are born,
Am ready for new mysteries,
I think of riding the bullock's horns

To sweaty dust; I climb Hermit's Peak
Ten thousand feet up beyond trees
Where in the last reaches high crosses
Mark the stages of the Penitentes.

Some say their savage mysteries
Were so guarded on the heights
That when a non-believer climbed to them
They slew him with a light slingshot.

Bluebells, bluebells, how frail and Spring-like,
Another world all fragile and intact,
O bluebells of the early memories and life,
A fair elixir before the killing facts.

The Inward Rock

When I had withdrawn into the uniqueness of rock
I assumed the inwardness of time.
I became rock: I was the rock and time
Living in pure events of eloquence.

I left great Caesar in the market place,
And heard the tyrants rise and fall
In jubilations of clashed syllables
That had no meaning at all.

Philosophers appeared to me in a dream
Whose advent made a pleasing sound;
Poets with their grave, synthetic eyes
Amazed the fronds to leap and bound.

The old hermit of Cape Rosier came
Who seventy years had stood at ease
By the side of the sea, with two black cats;
Saints finally smote him to his knees.

And that blind man who wove wicker chairs
All through the black and winter nights
To whom the world was as a peace
No others knew in their delights.

These appeared to possess the world,
And then a golden child of nine or ten‑
With light step under a golden head
Danced into the world of men.

But I had withdrawn into the uniqueness of the rock
Who sought impossible credulities.
I was rock and time: I had denied
The world to find poetic certainties.

So in the gift of silence, like the earth
Stable and defined in hardness and size,
I ventured into imaginative freedom,
In mystery, where truth is surprise.

An Evaluation under a Pine Tree, Lying on Pine Needles

When I wrote the abstract of Heaven
I felt worse, and went to a pine tree
Where I studied its fallen needles
To see the pattern of the universe.

When I had made love to woman
I felt moral, as having conquered this,
And kept faith with a mystical union
Which is the saving grace of the world.

When I begat children, I knew I had lived
And surrendered my fullness to the future.
But always there was a spirit in the flesh
That the flesh demanded greater sacrifice.

I hung on godhead all a strained life,
Wrestling with notions of the supernatural,
Craving the finite taste of infinite essence,
Believing in the glory of disbelief.

I came back to the wonderment of nature
Under a pine tree, my skin abraded by needles,
Affirming the great distillate of joy,
Walking in the woods, inevitable, evanescent.

54

When I was fifty years old, I felt
The grandeur of my volatile ignorance
And I made words as ruthless as an arrow
To pierce your heart with vigour and resonance.

Therefore let us rejoice, and though I offend
And there is no end of suffering,
Accept my song, be rich in my nature,
Bend to the northwind, and to the pine song.

Kaire

If I were Sophocles, brave with truth,
Writhing in the darkness of humanity,
Bright with an occluded brightness,
Able to hold in total mind
The fantastic reality of the human condition,
I wonder what I would have done
About a world beyond the Greek,
For he knew the zenith and nadir
Of passion, and he knew that beyond reality
Was the other passion of mythology,
That myths were sensual as tears or dreams,
The stains of error in the habit of truth,
Leaning beyond the flesh to the strength of the gods.

If I were Sophocles, ebullient and melancholy
Today, I would be unable to say
How far distant is the dream of Eros,
How divorced from primal concern seems truth,
How love is the power we but dimly see,
Love is that wholeness of the passionate mind
Glimpsed in the sensitivity of being;
The blind in our day see more than the seeing;
This is as the vessel in the enriching breeze
Knowing only immediately where the wind is blowing,
Yet time will take it to the mark
Eventually. Hear the lark
In its cry at dawn. Hear the stating
Breakers: before destruction they preserve you
To dream on a world of immortality.

57

The Struggle

Longing went out from him like a flag
Run up the mast of heavens. Rains were torn
From tremendous downpours. The careening ships
Strode in the chaos of the moral seas.
Everything
Was what it is not.

In the blasts of heavenly conjecture,
Maledictions crashing like tined thunderbolts,
The skies opened as in better centuries;
Mercy appeared, white-throated, visionary.
All would
Become what it is not.

Desire was against imperishable death,
A seed-bursting openness, an avenging
Unquenchable archangel, militant, consuming
The ether. Heaven defend the earth. All care
That love
Become what it is not.

The World Situation

I

I went out to meet the world,
My heart was light and gay.
The world turned gray and sour,
I had to flesh my fangs.

It was the inner imagination
I served. It was a purity of life
My innocence thought was tantamount
To the whole turmoil of strife.

I thought man had an honesty
Precluding malice. I felt the chill
Cold calculation of his evil,
The malevolence of his will.

In the force of my contention
I became a battleground.
Freedom, I cried, freedom of soul and light
And flailed my arms around

Until I quieted and pointed them hard
At my heart. There is your enemy,
There is the world's disparity.
Your better knew it in Gethsemane

I cried, whole decades of life
Filled with reality and brimstone.
I wanted to change the world.
My will was seated in the bone.

I could not change the world without,
I could not change the world within.
I live and breathe in a mortal quest,
Without, a dilemma; a red richness within.

II

Down in deep wells of consciousness
I fought the battle of mankind.
When I thought I saw the way
Then I was most blind.

I figured I could win
In the thickets of insurrection
By wit, decision and the volatile
The enemy banner's defection.

My assault was brutal and severe—
The forces joined were blue and gray.
My heart had a red force,
I fought all night and all day.

I fought for weeks, for years, a life.
I fought the battle of mankind,
Locked in a mortal embrace,
Seeing best when I was blind,

For then in deepest feeling alone
I felt the mighty assaults and defeats
Of man's struggle with the world,
His soul's flights, his animal heats,

The tragedy of his essence,
His agony and his pain,
The fury of the situation,
Man's follies that are vain.

I arose from meditation saying
In all this stupendous play
Let a little love into the picture,
Red love, at dawn, both light and gay.

III

Love appeared when killing most
Employed men locked in mortal harms.
They shed each other's blood
Locked in each other's arms,

Dealing death. The Devil laughed,
Giving them evil. They lusted after
Death and loved the Devil
And therefore loved their own disaster.

I saw them struggling on the plain,
Their bodies locked in bloody brightness,
A clotted mass, man in his essence,
To savagery gone, and mental lightness.

Then, as obscurely as fighting and the rest,
Love appeared over the horizon
In the form of woman, as redeemer,
Radiant in the sun's warming orison.

It was unbelievable but true
That the glory of this sight
Appeased the beast in man
And made him not fierce to fight.

61

He held to the glory of the world,
Color, tone, propensity, desire
When love entered into his heart,
Kindling compassionate fire.

He defeated evil, death, and battle
In love redeeming the human flesh,
Reddest love, innocent and experiential,
Which grows and fructifies the human wish.

A New England Bachelor

My death was arranged by special plans in Heaven
And only occasioned comment by ten persons in Adams, Massachusetts.
The best thing ever said about me   .
Was that I was deft at specifying trump.
I was killed by my father
And married to my mother
But born too early to know what happened to me,
And as I was an only child
I erected selfishness into a personal religion,
Sat thinking forty years saying nothing.
I observed all. I loved to drink gin,
Would not have thought to go farther
Into arcane episodes of the heavier drugs,
And, being New England, always remained sober.
However, I confess now, I was
Always afraid of women,
I don't know why, it was just the way it was,
I could never get very close to any woman.
Knowledge and intelligence allowed me
The grand rationalization of this; also, I respected
Delicacy, but would not go too far in any direction.
I thought I was a good man. I was.

I did not obstruct the state, nor religion,
But I saw through both and maintained my independence.
I kept my counsels among the learned.
My learning was more private and precious than worldly.
The world had no sense of the devious,
So my private vicissitudes were mine alone.

I say all this with a special sort of grace
For I avoided many of the pitfalls of fallen man
And while I did not have heroic size, the
Creative grandeur, or mastership of the mind
I earned my bread by cynicism alone,
And blow you all a kiss from the tomb.

A Maine Roustabout

Her was there as the yachts went by

Percy is my name; my accent is good,
I am told, as good as that of an Elizabethan.
I had no schooling beyond the age of sixteen.
My wife left me. I took to drink, live with a dog.
I resent children unless they can hold their own
With grown-ups. I've been around the world on ships,
Down Connecticut way on jobs, once got to Georgia,
Always return to the rocks and the hard times
Of Maine. At clambakes in the summertime
I sit with the summer folk on the conglomerate shore,
Play my old fiddle a sharp tune or two,
Old airs I learned from my brother when we were boys.
It was always tough with me. Sharp as the city folks
I think I am, but am ever wary against them,
Keep my difference, and will not let them tell me off.
I have no respect for their savage villainies,
Yet their power over life always fascinated me.
They own the place. They come and go, I'm left
To chores and dung. But I can catch a mackerel
Almost any afternoon on the incoming tide
With an old hook, when they're running, old line,
In my old boat: they won't take hook from the richlings.
If I scare the children with my grizzled face
It's an old gut forced with whiskey keeps me going.

Sea Burial from the Cruiser *Reve*

She is now water and air,
Who was earth and fire.

Reve we throttled down
Between Blake's Point and Western Isle,

Then, oh, then, at the last hour,
The first hour of her new inheritance,

We strewed her ashes over the waters,
We gave her the bright sinking

Of unimaginable aftermaths,
We followed her dispersed spirit

As children with a careless flick of wrist
Cast on the surface of the sea

New-cut flowers. Deeper down,
In the heavy blue of the water,

Slowly the white mass of her reduced bones
Waved, as a flag, from the enclosing depths.

She is now water and air,
Who was earth and fire.

66

A New England View: My Report

The men of Vermont were aiming at New Hampshire.
The men of New Hampshire were aiming at Vermont.
In the middle was a deer forced into the river.
He looked to the right, to the left, frightened, swam
Down the middle of the Connecticut river,
On a cold day in occlusive December.

It was a sight for the gods to behold.
The irony of his power was lost on the creature.
He displayed a fearful sense of his plight.
The deer faced death by drowning or by shot.
The men did not dare to raise their sights.
Such was the condition of the animal kingdom.

Flux

The old Penobscot Indian
Sells me a pair of moccasins
That stain my feet yellow.

The gods of this world
Have taken the daughter of my neighbor,
Who died this day of encephalitis.

The absentee landlord has taken over Tree Island
Where one now hesitates to go for picnics,
Off the wide beach to see Fiddle Head.

The fogs are as unpredictable as the winds.
The next generation comes surely on,
Their nonchalance baffles my intelligence.

Some are gone for folly, some by mischance,
Cruelty broods over the inexpressible,
The inexorable is ever believable.

The boy, in his first hour on his motorbike,
Met death in a head-on collision.
His dog stood silent by the young corpse.

Last week, the sea farmer off Stonington
Was tripped in the wake of a cruiser.
He went down in the cold waters of the summer.

Life is stranger than any of us expected,
There is a somber, imponderable fate.
Enigma rules, and the heart has no certainty.

Ruby Daggett

She, a woman of abrupt features,
Cocked an eye this way and that. Another
Decade went by. She sat still in her place,
Looking out at the alley from the bookstore.
She was the mistress of rich indices.
Who came, who went, who was in, who was out
She noted, impersonal above the day's charges.
Chocorua jumped from the cliff, the cash register struck.
Another decade passed, she sat erect.
Before she knew it another would come and go.
She, a woman of abrupt features,
In a small space, looking out at the alley,
Encyclopedic among files, ensconced,
Let vision flow over the peaks of time
As over the mountains of imaginative reality,
Watching the people and books come and go.
Ledyard cut his canoe, carved an archipelago.
She was like a peak. She was distant,
Who was always present. She was stalwart,
Like mountain silence. And she knew,
Take care of the day and the day will take care of you.
Roosevelt rolled up a ramp at Marlborough.
Ike beamed. Kennedy rolled up his sleeves on the green.
She knew the scent of books, as intimate as age.
In ink she suspected a waft of sage.

Hardening into Print

To catch the meaning out of the air
Yet have it inviolably there,
Life I mean, the glimpse of power, incomparable times
Of total splendor, the sudden exaltations,

Flash of a thrush, a rush of golden insight,
To be caught up in titanic light
As if one saw into the depths of things,
Yet averts the eye, to try yet further mysteries,

It is into this rich reservoir
Of knowing and unknowing I flash,
And shake high lightning spears of life
In the long combats of mortal strife,

Thrush song piercing human ills
With rigor and wrench so deep,
This glimpse is of an immaculate joy
Heart suffers for, and wishes to keep.

The Lament of a New England Mother

Where have I lost my way among money and horses?
My mind is like the keen edge of a blade.
I am a Bourbon of Vermont. My children are prickly in the wheat.
In the castle of torment I swing in the winds of chance.
Do I dare my Adversary to duty past delirium?
Do I mock the green ancestors in my recklessness?
Is there any recourse when death has taken my beloved?
That cancerous fiend has made my assertions vain.
The world is rocking that most stable was.
My estates panic in the trembling of my will.
I am the crossed and vexed one, the soiled evidence
Of universal malevolence, guilty to have been born,
To marry, to bear children, to affront Providence with spleen.
I am in search of a soul revolutionized.
When shall I see the pure stars of my childhood,
When shall I trust in the love of my pure husband?
When shall I unseat my selfishness, my false debate,
And live in the rich simplicity of the earth?
The world has visited me with viciousness
And all my life is humorless and viscid.
I cannot cope. I am the lost cornucopia
Of June. Yet I seethe with rebellion still,

Daunting society in the mazes of my perfidy.
Let me go, Fate, and bring me back to douceur.
The graveyard on the hill that holds the bones of my husband
Affrights me with the rancor of life. My lovers
Have all gone into the garden. My richness of fantasy
Plagues society; I am a checkerwork of secrets
Knocking together in a burden of black action.
Wring me when my hands were dry, Life,
You wrung. Despair is noncapitulatory.
The delicate psychiatrist has become more delicate
For dealing with me. I improve his uncertainties
As he drives me further to the absurd.
Why should he be able to unlock my balance?
I am his high price. I had never dreamed, in the green
Wonderwork spaciousness and grace of my Springtime,
That it would come to this graceless nightmare and fact.
No restraint. I am the naked ecstasy
Of Fate. I thought I had reserves of strength.
I have nothing to live for but endless night
Without stars, moon, lovers, or a dream of peace.
So do I dream of a heavenly Adversary
Who will take me to peace, and he is death,
I call him then sweet names, and pour out all my love
And take in my arms this impossible savior
As a result of the cruelty of reality.
How should I do else? I am corrupt and unforgiven.
I have lost the long battle with myself.
My children suffer, but I do not suffer more,
Having suffered too much in the death of my husband.
Let the ordeal of life confine itself
To graceless fantasies; I incorporated reality
In the beliefs and charms of our society.

My studious Vermont of the sage ancestors!
My riches, my great inheritance, my satisfactions!
One by one, in deep and subtle wrenches,
I am reduced. All the glory is taken away.
My mind itself, now struggling in the balance,
Teeters debile, in idiotic frenzies.
I know that I am keen in shrillness and immediacy.
I am gone to carelessness, and survive by chance.
For what? My deepest accusations seem petty,
O that lost loveliness of the ethereal!
Should my mother accost me, I shall say
I am a mother. If my children, what
Can I say? To go with one's father is over,
My husband was shaken from life like a seed.
I stand alone, driven out of Eden,
Knowledge too much for humankind.
I in my borderline, adept and side-stepping,
Have gone over to the snaky wilderness.
I am the force that whirls me serpentine.
I look my fate directly in the face.
A revolver within my paleness and hauteur,
I commit myself into the hands of the State.

Father and Son

Father   Could you catch a little fish, Son,
            Could you catch a little fish?

Son   Yes, Father, I could catch a little fish,
            A little fish, Father, catch,
            But I must do it in my own way.

Father   But I have got the proper hook, Son,
            I have got the proper book of hooks.

Son   Let me cast it my own way, Father,
            I will not get the line caught in the reel.
            Let me catch, Father, fetch the fish.

Father   Son, catch the fish the way I say, Son,
            Hold the line up fair and fine from the river.

Son   I have a bobbin, Father, I have a bobbin,
            See my bobbin swirling in the rapids, Father,
            I like to let my line down for the fish to see.

Father   Quickly, Son, pull the line in quick, Son.
            Don't be a laggard when the fish may pull.

Son	I will await my time, my time await, Father,
	I have never put my hook herein before,
	Let me, Father, let me dawdle by the shore.
Father	You've fouled the reel, Son, the reel already.
	Take out the bait and straighten, I'll help you straighten.
Son	But, Father, I have got to catch a little fish,
	I feel a fish is waiting under for my line.
	Let me do it my way, Father, my way.
Father	Leave the hook and bobbin in the swirling river
	And may you catch a little fish, a little fish today.
Son	They say they bite when there is nearly thunder.
	My crisp creel is waiting for the advent, Father,
	I want to net a vivid fish today.
Father	No doubt we have come here too late in the day.
	Son, come home, give up the quest, and come away.
Son	Such pleasure it is to dawdle by the river,
	I'll come if, come away if, come if, Father,
	If only a fish will bite upon my line.
Father	I said to pull your line in, pull, and come away.
	Pull in the bobbin, flat, and wind in the reel.
Son	If this is a command, Father, I'll come away.
	But fish must be in the river, fish for me.
	And if there are none for you, I'm sorry, Father, sorry.
Father	Then come, I'll take you home, you home, take,
	I'll take you safely from the rapids and the river.

76

Son   I'll catch the fish that you have never caught, Father.
        I'll catch the fish, bobbing fish, in my own way.
        If you will only wait and watch, and wait and see.

Father Some say the fish are endless in the sea.
        There is a spawn of life beyond our wills.

Son   My fish are what I wish to catch, Father, own fish,
        Now help me up the bank, me help, now help,
        Father. You brought me, now you take me back.

Father and Daughter

Daughter   Say it plainly, Father, say the sun is real.

Father   The sun has a fuzzy glow of yellow.

Daughter   I feel so joyful when I am in the sun.

Father   For me it has a menacing attitude.

Daughter   But why, Father, I can jump and leap in it.

Father   You have not been betrayed by time.
The sun is not necessarily good
And its glow is a presentiment of darkness.

Daughter   Be joyful, Father, for I am the sun's conqueror
As I skip on the grass and whirl my hoop
Around and around and around about my body.

Father   I admit I am your body, and you
Are my body and we live in the sun's gold body.
The eye is made for reality, not philosophy.

Daughter   Come, Father, and play in the yellow grass.

Father   Philosophy is not what changes the sun's color.

Daughter   Come, Father, and run with me now and here.

Father	You were veined, enmeshed in your young mother. I ran with you far back in the dark past.
Daughter	Do you see how striking, how flashing it is?
Father	I see partially through the gold of illusion But you do not know the passage of time I know. Therefore life is different from what I see.
Daughter	I can do three cartwheels in a row. Watch me.
Father	I have pondered the Father, the Son, and the Holy Ghost. I have thought of them as a fiction like your youth Which is immortal as you lithely turn on the grass.
Daughter	Do not tell me what I cannot understand.
Father	I have seen you as a process of being, Myself a process of being, and all being As a mysterious process of eternal becoming.
Daughter	The sun is thinning out beyond the pine trees.
Father	There is nothing like the splendor of late afternoon In September, before it is the end of September.
Daughter	Let me do a dance I made up, a yellow sun dance. I promise it will take only the shortest time.
Father	Yours is the shortest time. Your radiancy Will not stay, but my age will not stay either. It took me the longest time to learn my ignorance.
Daughter	There! Did you like it? Now I must go and play with my dolls.
Father	Dolls are for children. Suffering is for men. Laughter is for death.

The Lost

Most intimate, most far, most ethereally near,
It is you I write to, without a name,
Nameless and evocative and purposeful, blear,
Whose infinite life I esteem and claim:

It is you I hold most clear and most dear,
Most evocative and forever most pure and sure,
You who were destroyed by the rams of a tear,
For whom psychoanalysis had no prayer, no cure:

It is you who will read this in misery
I write for, you who may survive the volt fates,
And read the evolution of your stormy essence
As vessels diced and tolled in watery estates:

It is you who have escaped essential vainglory
And you who have trapped a final triumph of pride
At whose side in the purity of this clamant word
At the world's verge and judgment I rise, I ride:

It is you who drowning now were green with hope,
Whose life burst like a flare and dropped from sky,
Whose attitudes I espouse dark-heartedly:
It is for an impossible cause I would die.

Nameless my love, my loves, my many esteems.
It is all who are broken, who are nameless and reviled
I speak for in a language of the stalwart and kind,
In the redemption of forgiveness, as grace is to be mild.

You who were the image of the human fate,
You who shook, and you who arose and tried,
Who remember the savage depths of the world,
I speak for, reach. You shall not have died

Until each human heart lives for love alone
And every human spirit is enriched, occulted, blessed
With the hidden inherent spirit of the godhead,
Imperishable as the spirit of the possessed.

It is then, when love is victor and conqueror,
That, relaxing my revolution and astonishment,
Nameless my love, my loves, my many esteems,
I shall the gall, the spleen relax, take back, and repent.

Moment of Equilibrium
among the Islands

The sea repeats itself in light flourishes,
The southwest breeze-up of the midday
Is a lavish presentiment of possible danger,
Coves beckon as waves attack the prow
And slip past in stubby frenzies of loss.
Then we dare the open ocean; the green swells
We ride over with thorough, lordly motion,
Lovers of wind, sun, and the world-turn horizon,
And seek a new island, with a small spit of sand.
The anchor holds; we climb through contorted woods
Up boulders to an old granite quarry, whose
Dark, green, still, fresh water refutes the ocean.

It is the moment of looking down to still water
From massed granite blocks pleases the soul
With the hardness and fantasy of the world,
Before me must try again the gripping buoyancy
Of the salt sea, whose profound depths
Appear only to the imagination, while eyes
Survey the fresh roads the vessel walks
In triumph of buoyancy, delicacy, and strength,
As a philosopher continuing in the essential.
Then standing to the westward-closing sun
As the wind dies and waves grovel to stillness,
We reach at nightfall the landfall buoy of home.

Hark Back

To have stepped lightly among European marbles
Dwelling in a pantheon of air;

To have altered the gods in a fact of being;

To have envisaged the marriage
Of everything new with the old,

And sprung a free spirit in the world

Is to have caught my own spirit
On a bicycle in the morning

Riding out of Paris,
Heading South.

My flesh felt so good
I was my own god.

Am I My Neighbor's Keeper?

The poetry of tragedy is never dead.
If it were not so I would not dream
On principles so deep they have no ending,
Nor on the ambiguity of what things ever seem.

The truth is hid and shaped in veils of error
Rich, unanswerable, the profound caught in plain air.
Centuries after tragedy sought out Socrates
Its inexplicable essence visits us in our lair,

Say here, on a remote New Hampshire farm.
The taciturn farmer disappeared in pre-dawn.
He had beaten his handyman, but no great harm.
Light spoke vengeance and bloodstains on the lawn.
His trussed corpse later under the dam
Gives to this day no answer, says I am.

Christmas Tree

Up a heavy wooded hill
A brother and a sister go
As on a new adventure,
Climbing through a foot of snow.

Their faces shine; their axe is gleaming.
All morning seems to be their nurture.
They inspect the winter world
As if they were out to conquer nature.

Hand and helve now have their will.
They cut a Christmas tree from earth,
Two children shouldering home the trophy
To give the tree symbolic birth.

Then worshipping, not knowing,
With lights, and gauds, and gifts, they play
Lightly, in their youthful growing,
Nor climb to confront divinity.

Looking at the Stars

Hung up there in the sky,
The old pendant stars
In metallic blue night,
Cold and clear, neat in November,

Chaste, incredible and inscrutable,
I am their daft onlooker,
To whom a half a century of life
Is as a moment of this night.

They opened to me when I was young
Infinite spaces to my longing,
Inevitable portents of feeling
And blessed my growing and my knowing.

Now I must make my own myth
Among the myriad hard stars!
Now I must see them as false lights
Dependent on my subjectivity!

When I am not here to see them
May young lovers come and find
In the rubescence of their flesh
The sable and cold limits of the mind.

And let them bend together narrowly
Under the vastness before the daylight,
Cling together in the mortal lot,
Witness the beyondness of their sight

And say, All you who lived before us,
You to whom the stars were impenetrable,
They are mysterious to us too,
We relive an ancient ceremony

Of our unknowing and your unknowing
And see them chaste, infallible, white
In beds of blue, as now our love
Gives prescience and influence to the night.

Rainscapes, Hydrangeas, Roses and Singing Birds

Rain thunderstorms over the Potomac, in Georgetown,
Descend blistering June to the coolest aftermath
Of birds clamant, wet roses burgeoning to open
And airplanes hungering for the skies again.

I could not call it landscape. It is too intimate.
Here the lush nature of the summer world
Reads a strength of vines into any doubt,
States nature is hale despite the canting absolute.

Call to the caterpillar in furry brevity,
To the heavy bee dramatic over the tigerlily,
To the cardinal stripped of every perfidy,
To the cocktail party glancing from the glasses

And say that rainscapes, hydrangeas, roses and
Singing birds parade a splendor of late afternoon
In June in fleshtime in the saunter of early summer.
Children propel their skyey laughter to the future.

I am the proliferation of nature,
Non-political, affirmative, tumultuous,
I am the rainscape, hydrangeas, the rose and
The singing bird and bard, triumphing tumescent

In this hour of the earthly Paradise.
Opulence is as indifferent as death itself.
I would rather be and sing this positive hour
Than groan in nightscape nightmare makeshift error. Now

The storm is lifting and the pale, late, subservient sun
Salutes the skies with a rosy, infallible glow
Of delicate and parson-haunted ineffable benediction
As I think of my days in the earth, memory long aglow.

Dream Journey
of the Head and Heart

My head, so rarely rent
For all the rending time does me
Into a dreaming vortex went
To see what I could see.

I wanted to go down those steeps
Into a place of the unknown,
For surely, I thought, my head
Would save me with strong bone.

I went downward, circling wide
In cold, diminishing cones
Until, when far away from warmth,
I walked on bare and icy stones.

They were harsh but jewel-like, thrice
I tried to turn about and go
But the fascination of profundity
Urged me onward, swart and slow.

The strictures came with further travail
As inward came the walls and ribs,
More brilliant seemed the lights
In tossing, skeletal cribs

Illuminating darkness with strange rites
As my balked walk was probed.
Endlessly I seemed to stop
And now I was disrobed.

Head, ravenous intelligence,
Help me out of this thin place,
I cried, but nothing in the head
Caused radiance in the face

Until the heart, with pity of nothingness,
Woke in a dream of grace,
When I rose back into the world
On sufferance of the human race.

The Water-pipe

Do you remember, Bharati,
When you brought your water-pipe
From far, sepulchral India
To our evening in white-hot Cambridge?

A Princess among the intellectuals!
And your brown, brown flesh
Flashed under your Eastern sari?
I loved you subtly then, Bharati;

Unattainable Princess of India.
When I smoked your water-pipe,
Returning the stem, you would wipe
It carefully with a silken handkerchief.

But when you smoked my Western pipe
You grasped it and sucked in tobacco
As you would drink the West; nor wiped
The pipe stem, Bharati, Princess of India.

Winter Kill

Word traps catch big bears in silence.
They hunt the woods for years in freedom,
Keeping the counsels of the bees and snows.
Then, once unwary, a foot is caught in a trap.
The big black mountain comes atumble down.

His picture is put in the local paper.
The expressionless hunter stands in sullen pride;
A small son touches the nose of the brute.
The gun rests easy by the icy carcass;
People come to stare at the winter kill.

I would have him noble on the mountain side,
Roaming and treading, untrapped by man.
Man kills him only half for meaning,
Half out of thoughtlessness. The steaks
Are passed around as tokens to the neighbors.

Word traps catch big bears another way
When the meaning is total. The way a poem prinks
Into the heart from a forest hill
Is to have it in words, but never to have it.
Which is to say it is elusive still.

93

The Seal

A baby seal, shot by a hunter
Who should have known better, but out for pleasure,
I suppose, to get even with mean weather,
Saw no good blunter

Than killing an innocent thing.
The carcass rocked on the rocky beach,
On the flood tide, just within reach,
So we made of our arms a sling

And brought him home, a rare prize.
I never thought I would skin a seal
But we live in the realm of the real
And I have a small trophy likewise.

If still the long ocean tides
Held the seal in ocean strife
I should have thought better of life,
And better of man besides.

Later or Sooner

Whether sooner or later
Does not matter. I should late
Make some final statement
About man's fate.

But I am fiery-starred,
Burning in reality,
And therefore what I would say
Is not what I can be.

Too much, or too little,
Leaves something to be desired,
My ultimate fealty
To what life inspired.

May I bless the inexpressible
Beyond tooth and fang.
When man rose up, he loved,
And when he loved, he sang.

Eagles

Nature's secrets are ever subtle.
After every human failure
Still she astounds the eye
With natural majesty.

Inherent in the able day
Is a source so pure and keen
It overwhelms the senses
With the newly seen.

The newly seen that is ancient
And touches our deepest heart
Under the chords of remembrance
Where belief would leap and start.

I saw three bald eagles
Flying over Undercliff
In ancient majesty and power.
My heart leaped up stiff

At so tremendous a sight,
Those great, rare birds in search,
Their strange cries gutteral,
One on a dead tree perched,

Then in unison and swift flight,
As if purpose were absolute,
They flew passionate, inexorable,
And wheeled from my sight.

The Gesture

From the drama of horror and despair,
Out of the window, over the casket,
Young girls are bringing spring flowers
Carried and proffered in a spring basket.

So light a gesture in so grave a time.
I am one who, flailed and threshed,
Wishes in his power to understand
What it is that death refreshed.

An intimate gesture of young girls.
The flowers are laid before her white face.
In the mystery of their understanding
Reposes what we know of grace.

The Master Image

The years were a glimpse of something undefined.
They obscured as much as they revealed. Tined
Hay tossed up. Why a girl died in a day.
Would a master image spring in the heart,

The elusive and incredible mystery?
Molasses and water for the hot hay-pitchers.
A broken-down hearse seeks the harsh rocks.
The changing people cannot see the centuries.

I saw a buck and two does leap
In silhouette against the cliff at dusk.
If I had a great grandchild,
Who am not yet a grandfather,

Would he see the picture? Static
Emblem of all animal change,
Fixed reality, world emblazonment,
As, pent in a poem, its bounding phrase.

The Diver

Where others dared not he would go,
They stood by fearful as he went under,
What rectitude, what inner mastery
Was in those dives blue, cold, and slow,

What was the wish of his tenacity,
What dark gods would he loose and plunder
As others watched, there where the source
Was masked in a dual obscurity,

Down in the depths of murk and rage
To fret and work the image of an age,
There in a silence vast and planless,
In the watery depths that are manless,

They saw him descend and reascend
And descend again, and again disdain
The advice of air and the stare of cloud
In repeated triumphs that cried aloud,

But he would slip off the white ship
And, struggling down in danger and flashing
A sign soon lost at the parted lip
Be gone under waves that are lashing

The waters of this world to seeming.
He dared to lose the world for meaning
Lurking in the depths so blue, so cold.
The truth, never old, the spectators never told.

To a Poet
Who Has Had a Heart Attack

Dear Poet, your heart is not in question.
Your heart was attacked long ago.
Long ago you were a sensorium.
It is only now that you are slow.

Now you lie on a hospital bed,
Your rich poems singing in your head,
Your life hanging by a thread,
The bulletins that you were almost dead.

Dear Poet, your heart is not in question.
It is the momentous question of poetry
That is loosing itself to be free,
Struggling toward immutability

In the great hurls and trials of the free,
In green dells, in finest beliefs,
In august solitudes of the heart,
In deaths of thought, through mankind's griefs.

Ultimate Song

It is too late for the ambiguous thrush
To sing in our garden, unseen though telling;
His wordless song, indescribably rich,
We cannot go on guessing in describing.

Nor flash his meaning back to China
Where love sat to a two-stringed instrument;
Nor bend to a blue tall night of Arabia
Where imagination feasts on the pomegranate;

Also, the Egyptian tombs are fragrant and dry
With aromatic spices of planned immortality;
The fallacy of duration is their stone spell,
Who felt eternity in sand, Nile, and sky.

Nor can the song of the mysterious thrush
Take us to England, whose elusive nightingale
Pre-empts many efforts to discover her there,
Though the searching heart think never to fail.

No, may the thrush among our high pine trees
Be ambiguous still, elusive in true song,
Never or seldom seen, and if never seen
May it to my imperious memory belong.

Vision

I

Two hummingbirds as evanescent as
Themselves
Startled me at my study window
As sea bells

Heard slipping through the fog,
Or yells
Of children down the block.

Phenomena,
Prolegomena,
They were

So sensitively sent
Beyond my pane,
Seen through it,

I thought the hummingbirds were angels
In a world of morning
And flowers
Soon invisible.

II

Again they come
Two hummingbirds,

But my eye,
Prejudiced to angelic vision,

Saw them not as brown,
Which they were, brown machines;

They riffle and rifle the flowers,
Sense-drenched in September;

Sense-drenched I exult
In their lithe bodices—

Where will they go, above
The frail duration of a flower,

Powerful in frailty,
Come October, come November?

III

The hummingbirds of hope!
Hope they are of all
That is exquisite and beautiful,

Small, round, and smooth,
Burke's three categories for the beautiful,
Held in an instant

Before the eye which triumphs
In realization and sings
Insistence all through the being

Of the rich delight of this seeing,
Sings of purity and power,
And hope that is highest

When visions of the earth
Like intuitions before birth
Sing, sing with the hummingbirds.

103

May Evening

Long after our departure
Someone in a moment of significant rapture,
Seeing a boy beside a fountain,
Watched by an elder in a garden,
Will think that the past is the future
And the present is both.

We live in the imagination of the moment
When in a harmonious instant of apprehension
Subtle dreams are reality.
A boy playing by a fountain, unselfconscious,
A man watching him, studious in a garden,
Partake of immortality.

I am my father's father, or farther back,
Some enchanted man of the twelfth century;
I am Socrates' questioner in the agora,
I am a child dancing on the green seen by Blake,
I am all those to whom a moment has meant
A spell of rapture and a gift of grace.

The boy deploys from the playing water,
The man with his visions goes to get some coffee,
The incredible elan of the springtide evening
Lingers but departs; the graceful salute of the static
Moment of happiness and concord is given.
Fate outlasts the flash. Recognition was on us.

Death by Drowning

His guitar was found in the canoe on the river
But cold grappling hooks brought his body up from the deeps.
He was a young man introduced to death by a gust.
They were upset by the nature wildness keeps.

Unbelievable, fierce, eternal, high wind in clear air
Tossed three youths; the boat escaped downstream.
One met the brutal grip of the cold, hands of ice
Pulled him down; the others barely made it to life's dream.

His guitar was found in the canoe on the river,
O unbelievable! May all the gay songs of youth
Assuage, if they can, the brutal indifference of fate.
His companions live to ponder on death's truth.

Ways and Means

I fight with the tools of the mind
But I love with the love of a lamb.
I believe in the objective world
To find out what I am.

I laugh at wolf-circling death
Because I know he is closing in;
No matter what stance I take
He will always win.

Will win! But I will abuse
His privilege with love of poetry;
Its power put on, and use
The subtle songs of immortality.

Meditation One

The body tires of the nonsense of the world.
Where is the sense?

In the cartwheel of my daughter.
In the football catch of my son.

In blackouts, doubts, inabilities, horrors.
In the very indeterminations of our sense.

The body tires, but the mind follows illusion.
The mind is indefatigable while the body lives.

It is the mind that conceives glory and cunning
And soars aloft at the slightest, sweep promptings.

If I were to sing the mind, I would sing
The resolute assumptions of prime difficulties

And I would bless the eagle soaring in the heavens
From a predisposition to height and sun-likeness.

If there is a fiction of the flesh, a lassitude
Engendered by years of hoeing the earth,

Is there not an equal fiction of the mind
Pondering Plato and Aristotle, who said all between them,

Or so it is said in our time, a fiction of possession,
For how can we allow these old men to rule our garden,

And if there is a fiction of the body and of the mind,
Where then is reality? Is it at Harvard? At Lagos?

I in a baffled clarity of unassimilated absolutes,
Which is to say a pleasure of archaic riches,

Sense where we start again
After living in the confines and starts of nonsense.

We begin with the belief in a great mother,
The motherwater and ancient, grand indestructibility

Of birth-thrust, and in this mystery remaining alive
We are the eager champions of onrushing time

Which we take in arms like an irresistible lover,
And have the world as in our time. Then the dearth

Of nature easily assailing our senses confronts us
With the inevitable and fast-coming knowledge of death,

Perplexing to aspiration, and so deep a charge
As to acknowledge the essence of our being.

Then where shall we go? And to whom apply?
Who but to God the anchor of man's vanity,

For I have aforesaid our stability
In gardens of growth, and a wise insouciance,

But then we are perplexed in furtive enigmas,
Distracted in feats and assonances of fates,

And we, in the peregrine style of full acquiescence,
Engage furor, belay our dangerous drops,

And think we have Heaven indeed in hand,
Think we have Hell safely under our belts,

But to God we have incontestably to go,
We have to announce him as we pale in flesh,

And to His Son our Saviour bow knee and give service,
When in folly of mind we see the folly of mind.

The dogged New England American, trumped at last,
Has his hand taken by a god in the underbrush,

As it were, and has to admit glorious intrusion
On his own pain and comforts of the rational mind

And thus lean to poetry as a canorous canticle
And high diapason Godward sent, impelling him

To delicate, time-defeating elaborations
Of the deepest serenities of the heart and mind.

For of all we have learned in a life of effort
Most we have learned is that we know little,

While in natural humility, able to envy our senses,
We are yet able to see another point of view,

To worship the rose window of Palma de Mallorca,
Or be breathless before Ilaria del Caretto.

I began on nonsense and I end on sense,
Which is the wish of man to cultivate the world's garden,

Give the Devil his due, praise God for invented Heaven,
And hold to the end every last thing in view.

Meditation Two

Style is the perfection of a point of view,
Nowise absolute, but held in a balance of opposites

So that for a moment the passage of time is stopped
And man is enhanced in a height of harmony.

He has purchased at a great price the gems of elan
In some avid precinct of his personality,

The price of years of doubt and belief, of suffering
The enigmas of the day, every hardy opposition

Of opinion, and every gain of hard-constructed good,
Music of furor, or insights passive and sovereign

When the clearest dreams are in a half-lit wakefulness,
When the best love is untutored, able to be blessed.

It is the style of the mariner proud on his vessel,
Who keeps a weather eye to the storm, but hopes,

Aware of the improbable, weather will not alter
From gentle zephyrs allowing him the spectacle of July

As if the afternoon were perfect and endless,
Porpoises in pairs follow the ship, and seals

Poke up their hopeful heads to see what trespasses.
The lobsterman is still at pulling his traps,

And far off the race jockeys on its summer errands,
Lightly touched with an ethereal evanescence,

Before returning to the home clubhouse and yacht club,
Inevitably pulling down the small sails at nightfall.

So should reality seem to be a style
Consummate and faultless, held in the hand

As the tooled wheel before the magnetic compass,
And all should be orderly in earth as in heaven.

But that we know the gale will rive us,
Years cut down our vanities, time unseam us,

Force throw the weak baby seal to death
On the rocks, the unexpected shock sink the vessel,

Or worse, to see the oncoming rollers and savage tempest
And know our doom forced against any wood or canvas,

Where is the style then for man the master of earth
And of waters, man who thinks to control his life

And to roam through the black new wastes of space
As if he had comfort in his small, cramping capsule?

Is there an outer misadventure or foul catastrophe
So malign as the malevolent sunderings of the soul?

For down in the depths of the heart's adventure
The evil in man since the loss of Paradise

And that knowledge which came in the Garden of Eden
When Eve offered man the fruit of the womb and of life

Has taken every stride with his heavenward hope
And locked his going in his ever knowing dualism,

So that from the opposites of good and evil, flesh and spirit,
Damnation and redemption, he is never absent

But truly is fixed in a vise of these opposites
Contending manly, forcing his sperm on children,

Unable not to start the chain of being again,
Crying out again and again when he sees suffering.

Is it not a provocation of the spirit of unity,
That, despite the ramifications of disparate phenomena,

Man seizes immortality on the instant
And can make his watery flesh seem permanent

In the magical power of a given poem,
In the working of paint, in the modelling of stone,

In the flash and controlled passion of music,
Is not the style of the man caught in his art,

And is art itself not a triumph of nature,
Before the worm takes over, before the breakneck tomb?

I sing the harmony of the instant of knowing
When all things dual become a unity,

The power of the mind to envisage singleness,
The purpose of the hand to shape lovingness.

If I sing Aeschylean right-mindedness,
It is of myself mostly that I sing,

Hoping the improbable advent of unity
Will triumph over the mocking dualisms

Which, each seeming real, yearly tore me
In the macerations of their blooded factions

As, whether to fly out, and shout with the government,
Or, silent as a crab, burrow in the sands of solitude;

Whether to embark upon the waves of chance,
Or reside in some closed nook of contemplation;

Whether to accept the brotherhood of the many,
Or live for the talents and the truths of the few.

So should style amplify and refine man's poise,
Be an instrument as lucid as the best of his knowing.

114

ॐ